FIRST IMPRESSIONS

FIRST IMPRESSIONS ·

Michelangelo

RICHARD McLANATHAN

Harry N. Abrams, Inc., Publishers

SERIES EDITOR: Robert Morton
COPY EDITOR: Patricia Gilchrist
DESIGNER: Joan Lockhart
PHOTO RESEARCH: Neil Ryder Hoos

Library of Congress Cataloging-in-Publication Data
McLanathan, Richard B. K.
     Michelangelo / Richard McLanathan.
     p.   cm. — (First impressions)
     Includes index.
     Summary: A biography of the Renaissance sculptor, painter, architect, and poet, whose
greatest work may have been the Sistine Chapel in Rome's St. Peter's Cathedral.
     ISBN 0-8109-3634-8
     1. Michelangelo Buonarroti, 1475–1564—Juvenile literature.
2. Artists—Italy—Biography—Juvenile literature. [1. Michelangelo Buonarroti, 1475–1564.
2. Artists.]   I. Title. II. Series: First impressions (New York, N.Y.)
N6923.BSM37   1993
700'.92—dc20
[B]   92–27688
Text copyright © 1993 Richard McLanathan
Illustrations copyright © 1993 Harry N. Abrams, Inc.

CHAPTER I

Finding His Way

"If I am good for anything," Michelangelo once told a friend, "it is because I was born in the good mountain air . . . and suckled among the hammers and chisels of the stonecutters." He was recognized early in life for his skill in carving stone. But the reference to stonecutters and their tools suggests more than

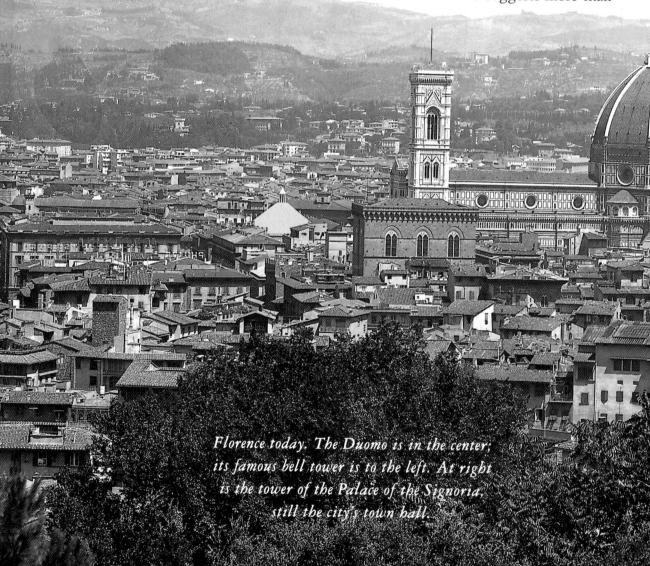

Florence today. The Duomo is in the center; its famous bell tower is to the left. At right is the tower of the Palace of the Signoria, still the city's town hall.

the mastery of a craft learned during a boyhood spent in a quarryman's household. It also suggests something of his basic approach to art. As an artist, he was essentially a sculptor. Not the kind of sculptor who models a figure to be cast in bronze or who creates a work by the assembly of parts, but the kind of sculptor who cuts and chisels away the extra material to free the form that, in his imagination, lies imprisoned within the block of stone.

Michelangelo's beginnings were far from promising. The second of five sons, he was born in 1475 into an aristocratic family, the Buonarroti Simoni. The family had risen to prominence more than two centuries earlier, but by the time of Michelangelo's birth, it was sadly in decline. There was little money and almost all the family property had been lost. All that was left was a

share in a house in Florence and a small farm near Settignano, a village famous for its stone quarries, situated a few miles east of Florence up the valley of the Arno River. Michelangelo's father, Lodovico, was a vain and shallow man who was too proud to work in any capacity except public office because he felt it was beneath his station in life to be a merchant or a farmer. Michelangelo's mother, Francesca, had married young and was overwhelmed by the constant demands of her selfish husband. There is no evidence of creativity or artistic ability anywhere in Michelangelo's family background. But there is no accounting for genius. Through some happy fortune he became the man his admiring contemporaries recognized as "Il divino Michelangelo." In their minds only divine inspiration could account for his extraordinary gifts. As his life progressed, their opinion seemed to be confirmed by a series of fortunate events that charted its course as if following a preordained plan.

Late in 1474, a few months before Michelangelo's birth, his father was appointed to a six-month term as governor of two remote little hill towns, Caprese and Chiusi, situated near the eastern boundary of Florentine territory. They lie in a mountainous region of steep slopes, abrupt cliffs, swift-flowing streams, rocky ravines, and dense forests of pine and beech trees. Lodovico and Francesca set out from Florence with their first child, Lionardo, who was about eighteen months old. The journey, though not long by modern standards, took several days because of the roughness of the countryside. The road was mostly a narrow, stony track, fit only for traveling on foot or on horse- or mule-back. There were few settlements, since most of the district was too rugged even for farms, vineyards, or olive groves.

The trip was particularly difficult for Francesca, who was pregnant. Finally the family reached Caprese and settled into the cold, drafty, partly ruined castle that was to be their home for the next six months. There, on March 6, 1475, Michelangelo was born, as he said, "in the good mountain air." He was christened two days later in the church of St. John in the village below the castle.

Within a few weeks, Lodovico's term as governor was up and the family returned to Florence. Francesca proved incapable of nursing Michelangelo, so he was sent off to Settignano to live with the family of a stonecutter whose wife became his nurse. For the next several years, he lived mostly with his foster family, making only occasional visits to Florence.

When Michelangelo was six, his mother died, worn out by child-bearing, and his connections with his father and brothers became even more distant. It

The castle in the mountains of Caprese, where Michelangelo was born.

was only after his tenth birthday, when his father married again, that he was summoned back to the family house in Florence.

The boy had already learned to use the tools of a stonecutter. With steel chisels and a hammer he could shape stones for buildings, rough out blocks for sculpture, and carve moldings and other decorative details. It was all laborious handwork, and even a small mistake could ruin hours or even days of hard and exacting toil. But while Michelangelo had mastered the stonecutter's craft, and his muscles were well hardened by the process, he could neither read nor write, skills that most Florentine boys half his age had acquired. Despite his stubborn resistance to academic studies, after three years of heroic effort by a dedicated tutor he became literate in Italian and picked up some Latin and Greek, then considered essential for an educated person.

Although this period of schooling was of limited success, Michelangelo did discover that he had a gift for drawing. He drew and sketched as much as he could, often at the expense of mathematics, grammar, and his other formal studies. He copied figures from paintings and sculptures he found in churches and soon developed a love for the arts. He also, in one of those happy circumstances that gave pattern to his life, became friends with Francesco Granacci.

Florence in the sixteenth century, looking up the valley of the Arno River. At the center is the cathedral, known as il Duomo for its towering dome by Brunelleschi. The narrow, battlemented tower of the Palace of the Signoria is to the right of the cathedral.

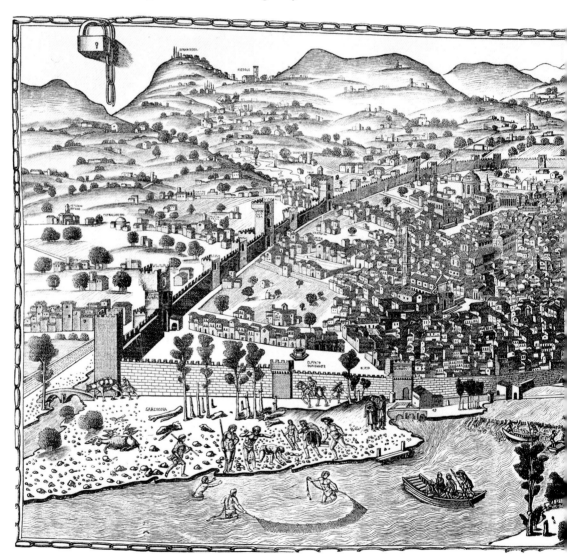

Granacci, who was a few years older, was already apprenticed to a leading Florentine painter of the period, a much respected man named Ghirlandaio. Ghirlandaio had a large workshop where he employed a number of assistants and several apprentices who had been placed by their families with him to learn the trade. All were kept busy by the flow of orders for altarpieces for churches, monasteries, convents, and private chapels. The shop also produced portraits of important people, or those who considered themselves important. In addition, Ghirlandaio's assistants decorated marriage chests and other pieces of furniture with appropriate scenes from the Bible or, as was increasingly fashionable, with amorous or warlike episodes from Greek and Roman myths.

Through Granacci, Michelangelo was introduced to the lively and active life of artists and patrons. He knew that he had found his calling. At the age of thirteen, with Granacci's encouragement, the boy informed his father that he, too, wished to become apprenticed to Ghirlandaio.

It says much for Michelangelo's determination that at thirteen he could face a person as unimaginative and unsympathetic as his father with a request that he knew would seem outrageous. His father's only interests were family and money. His only hopes were that his sons would restore the family fortune to assure that he, Lodovico, could live the kind of life to which he believed himself entitled. Here was a promising boy who wanted to throw it all away

St. Peter.
About 1492–93. When he was in his teens, Michelangelo made this drawing by copying a detail from Masaccio's fresco of about 1425, the Tribute Money, in Santa Maria del Carmine, Florence.

by becoming an artist. If there was anything that Lodovico held in contempt, it was the arts, along with those misguided and irrelevant people who produced them. Furthermore, he considered Michelangelo's announcement a betrayal of family. Little did he know that he was up against a greater force of character than he could hope to overcome. Despite frequent beatings and endless lectures, Michelangelo stood by his guns. Eventually, in a state of disgust that continued throughout his unhappy life, Lodovico gave in. He never understood or respected his son's gifts.

On April 1, then, in 1488, Michelangelo became apprenticed to Domenico Ghirlandaio. Through Ghirlandaio's shop he entered the world of the arts, his natural home, which he was to occupy with the greatest distinction for the rest of his long life. He must have felt a great relief. Since, as an infant, he had been put out to nurse with the stonecutter's wife, Michelangelo had never had a home with his own family. He had scarcely known his unfortunate mother, and he had nothing whatsoever in common with his father or his brothers. Now, living in Ghirlandaio's house and working in his shop, the boy found people young and old who shared his interests and understood his hopes and aims.

Michelangelo seems to have carried the wound of his emotionally deprived childhood throughout his life. This early deprivation is probably the reason he sought perfection with such determination. It may also explain why he was never satisfied with his achievements, even though people of his own day—as have those of all periods ever since—hailed them as works of genius. In his drive to prove himself to his uncaring father, he repeatedly took on more commissions than even he could handle and reproached himself when he could not complete them all. Having been thrown on his own so early in life, he often felt lonely and ill at ease with others and was often suspicious of their intentions. Being himself a perfectionist, he was impatient with anything that seemed to him slipshod. He drove himself relentlessly, often sleeping in his clothes a few hours at a time so he could put in many more hours of labor. Yet he was loyal to his friends and was a charming and witty companion to those with whom he felt at ease. And always he was a passionately patriotic Florentine, which brings us to another of those fortunate circumstances that informed his life—that he was born a citizen of Florence.

CHAPTER II

Lorenzo the Magnificent

The very name, Italy, was not often used in Michelangelo's time. The peninsula nation that today we call Italy was then made up of some fourteen separate states, more often at war with one another than at peace. They ranged from the republic of Genoa, the duchy of Milan, and the republic of Venice in the north to the kingdom of Naples in the south. In between were various other states, including the republics of Florence and Siena, the duchies of Ferrara and Modena, and other smaller political entities, most of which were ruled by petty tyrants. In addition there was the large domain governed by the pope from Rome, reflecting his status in those days as an absolute political ruler with formidable military power as well as a spiritual leader.

Democracy as we know it was unknown. The so-called republics were ruled by governing bodies elected not by the people but by the power structure of the community. In Florence, this power structure was the system of guilds, organizations which were similar to trade unions. The guilds were made up of merchants, tradesmen, and bankers, groups that had replaced the old feudal nobility of the Middle Ages.

Florence was a prosperous place, a crossroads for commerce and banking. During the city's heyday, Florentine banks financed most of the wars of Europe, lending money to kings and princes from England and Scandinavia to France and Hungary; to rulers in Italy including the pope; and to the Holy Roman Emperor, one of the most powerful political figures in Europe. The Florentine banking families had branches in most of the major cities. The Medici, for example, had representatives in Rome, Pisa, Venice, and Milan in Italy; in Avignon and Lyons in France; in Geneva, Switzerland; in Bruges, Belgium; and in London, England. Their Rome branch handled most of the business affairs of the papacy, including the profitable collection of papal revenues abroad. This not only made them a great deal of money, but also gave them great prestige and made them highly influential in international affairs.

The Medici had been the leading family in Florence for several genera-

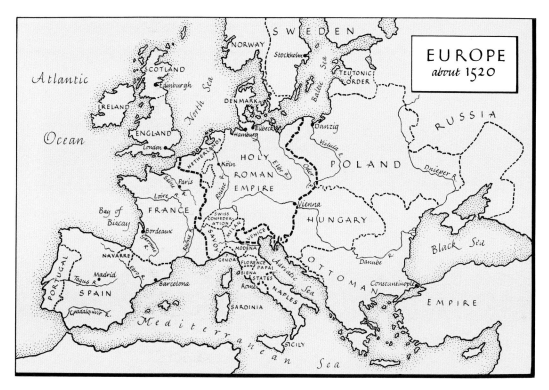

Europe in Michelangelo's day. While Spain and France were integral kingdoms, and greater Germany was under the control of the Holy Roman Emperor, Italy consisted of many independent states.

tions. In addition to being successful businessmen, they were also among the greatest collectors of the period of works of art, books, and manuscripts. They endowed and built hospitals, churches, monasteries, convents, and libraries, and they could always be counted on to contribute to worthy causes. Though they were virtual rulers of Florence, the Medici never interfered with the mechanisms of republican government because the Florentines were extremely sensitive about their rights as free citizens of an independent state. The Signoria, the city's governing body, whose membership was elected by the guilds, was largely controlled by friends and supporters of the Medici. The head of the family was often called upon for advice, especially in foreign affairs. Cosimo de' Medici, who died in 1464 in his seventy-sixth year, was the first to gain an international reputation. He played his role so discretely and effectively that his fellow citizens voted to have his tomb inscribed Pater Patriae, "father of his

Veduta della Piazza, e Chiesa di S. Giovannino de PP. Gesuiti,

country." Pope Pius II, an old friend, remembered Cosimo as "a king in all but name and state."

Cosimo was succeeded by his eldest son, Piero. He was known as Piero the Gouty because of the extreme severity of the arthritis that afflicted him—a condition which caused his death after only a few years as head of the family. Piero's courage was unquestioned, but he lacked something of his father's executive ability and tact. He died too soon really to prove himself.

On Piero's death in 1469, his older son, Lorenzo, was suddenly elevated into a position of leadership at the request of a committee of six hundred citizens. Lorenzo was just twenty, and his brother, Giuliano, was four years younger. Both were very young to occupy the positions of trust that they inherited. But people's lives were generally shorter in those days, and they grew up earlier. Michelangelo

The Medici palace, shown here in a drawing of about 1700 by Giuseppe Zocci, was the first great family palace of the Renaissance, begun in 1444 by Cosimo de' Medici, probably to plans by Brunelleschi.

decided on the course of his life at the age of thirteen, and Lorenzo de' Medici proved capable of being a head of state at twenty.

Lorenzo was better fitted for the position than his father had been. He had inherited his grandfather's diplomatic sense, and instinctively assumed the position of head of the family and leading citizen. He was always respectful of the Florentines' fear of the tyranny that prevailed throughout most of the rest of Italy. Both he and Giuliano were very popular, being lively, intelligent, polite, and approachable. Both were excellent athletes and expert horsemen. Unlike some of the aristocrats of the period, they had received a good Florentine education. They could read and write in their own language as well as in Greek and Latin. They knew history, classical literature, and music. Giuliano, to be sure, took such matters more lightly than his elder brother, who was a dedicated student of letters and of philosophy. Lorenzo was already a patron of the arts and a collector. He enjoyed the company of artists and scholars, and invited a number of them to live in the huge Medici palace. It was rather like a modern apartment house inhabited by many members of the same family and their friends.

Lorenzo and his friends met often, frequently inviting visiting scholars and poets to join the group. They took meals together, and discussed all sorts of things. Like so many others of the time, particularly in Florence, they found beauty and truth in the newly rediscovered world of ancient Greece and Rome. Because of their shared interest in the writings of the ancient Greek thinker Plato, Lorenzo's group came to be called the Platonic Academy. But don't let the formality of the name fool you into thinking that their meetings were serious and dull. Those who took part in the discussions were lively, bright, and congenial companions, and their conversations were witty and often humorous. They all enjoyed music, and several, like Lorenzo, composed songs which they played on the lute, a guitar-like instrument, or the lyre, a small harp. Some of Lorenzo's popular songs, mostly about love and the shortness of youth, are still sung in the streets of Florence. Those in Lorenzo's circle were serious, however, about one subject—the ideas of Plato. They were especially interested in

An unknown painter made this portrait of Lorenzo the Magnificent in about 1485. In the background is a panorama of Florence. The laurel tree at left makes a punning reference to the name of the sitter.

Sandro Botticelli. **Adoration of the Magi.** *About 1475.*
Botticelli's painting depicts members of the Medici family in the biblical
scene: Cosimo kneels to the left of the Virgin; his son, Piero the Gouty,
robed in red, kneels in the center. Lorenzo, Piero's son, wearing
a dark jacket, is at middle right. His brother, Giuliano, stands
at the far left beside the horse.

20

Plato's theory that the study of things that are truly beautiful and admirable leads one to an increased understanding of the basic truths that underlie the surface appearance of things. They would have agreed with the words of the great English poet John Keats who centuries later wrote that "beauty is truth, truth beauty."

The group also admired and collected the statues, coins, and manuscripts of ancient Greece and Rome. They studied the remains of classical architecture that still existed, the noble ruins of temples, bridges, tombs, and aqueducts scattered across the face of Italy, especially in and around Rome. Looking back through the gloom and disorder of the Middle Ages, from which their own times were just emerging, that remote past seemed ideal, sunlit, and glorious. They knew that they were living in a similar time of rebirth and renewal. The name that has been given to their period in history, the Renaissance, literally means "rebirth." These Florentines identified their city, the cradle of the Renaissance, with ancient Athens, the vital center of the classical Greek world, looking on Florence as the new Athens. Deeply religious Christians, they saw similarities between the ideal truths of Plato and the truths of Christianity. They identified that force that Plato recognized as giving order to the world with the God of the Bible. This imaginative linking of the best of the classical world with that of the Christian is basic to an understanding of the Renaissance. It underlies every aspect of Renaissance life, including the arts. It is central to the art and life of Michelangelo.

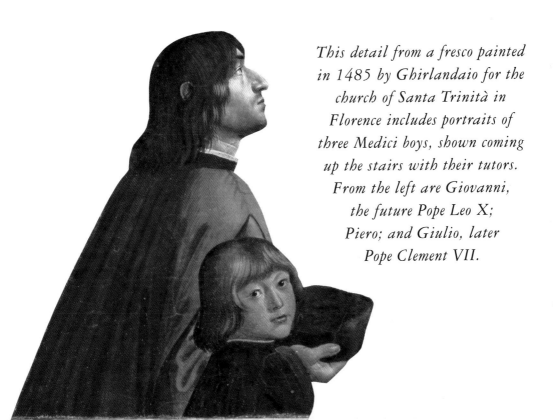

This detail from a fresco painted in 1485 by Ghirlandaio for the church of Santa Trinità in Florence includes portraits of three Medici boys, shown coming up the stairs with their tutors. From the left are Giovanni, the future Pope Leo X; Piero; and Giulio, later Pope Clement VII.

CHAPTER III

The Fall of the Medici

Michelangelo had just passed his fourteenth birthday when another fortunate event took place. In the summer of 1489, Lorenzo de' Medici invited an experienced sculptor, Bertoldo di Giovanni, to become keeper of the Medici collection of antique sculptures in the Gardens of San Marco, a small park near the Medici palace. There, Greek and Roman statues, architectural fragments, stone inscriptions, and various other objects from the classical past were displayed under trees and among shrubs and flowers. In addition to his duties as keeper, Bertoldo was to train promising young sculptors. Lorenzo asked Ghirlandaio to recommend young men to become Bertoldo's pupils, and Ghirlandaio sent two of his apprentices, Granacci and Michelangelo.

Years later, Giorgio Vasari, the great biographer of Italian artists, who was a pupil and lifelong friend of Michelangelo, wrote an account of what took place when the new students arrived. Michelangelo was given a chunk of marble to work on and carved the head of a faun, a minor nature god of the Romans, adapting it from an antique fragment in the collection. He did it so swiftly and so well, Vasari wrote, that Lorenzo, greatly impressed, "sent for Lodovico, Michelangelo's father, and formally arranged to receive Michelangelo into his princely household." Lorenzo gave him "an allowance of money and a purple cloak to wear, while his father, Lodovico, was made an official of the customs." Another friend of Michelangelo, Ascanio Condivi, noted that Lodovico "complained loudly that Lorenzo wanted to lead his son astray . . ." and was only most reluctantly persuaded to consent to his request.

Lorenzo treated Michelangelo like one of the family. The artist studied

***Madonna of the Stairs.** About 1491. This marble plaque was carved by Michelangelo soon after he was enrolled in the school for sculptors established by Lorenzo the Magnificent.*

with the Medici children, including Lorenzo's son Giovanni, a boy of his own age, and Giulio, son of Lorenzo's brother, Giuliano. Giovanni later became Pope Leo X, and Giulio became Pope Clement VII. Lorenzo invited Michelangelo to join in family activities, including their favorite diversions, poetry readings and improvising lyrics to the accompaniment of the lute. Lorenzo was one of the leading poets of his generation, and his great friend Politian, the boys' tutor, was another. The enthusiasm of Lorenzo's circle was catching, and Michelangelo's earlier lack of interest in letters vanished as another new world opened up to him. He learned by heart poems by Dante and Petrarch, the two pioneers who, over a century earlier, had composed some

Battle of the Centaurs. 1492. Michelangelo carved this relief just before his patron, Lorenzo the Magnificent, died.

of the world's greatest poetry, writing in their native Italian rather than in the previously preferred Latin or Greek. Michelangelo started to write sonnets of his own, poems that his elders found full of promise.

In about 1491, with Lorenzo's encouragement and Bertoldo's guidance, Michelangelo carved a thin, upright plaque, the *Madonna of the Stairs*, in marble. It is in the very shallow relief that the Italians call squashed relief, so described because there is very little difference in actual depth between the highest areas and the deepest ones. Yet there is an effect of space extending back from the foreground. The work is only a little more than twice the size of this page, and less than two inches thick, but the stairs recede as they rise upward. The Virgin's draperies are fully modeled; the figures firmly rounded.

A year later he finished the *Battle of the Centaurs*, in which he depicted those mythological figures that are half-man and half-horse. This work is also in marble. It is somewhat larger in size than the *Madonna of the Stairs* and is carved in much higher relief. The subject, suggested by Politian, is from a Greek myth. But more important than the story is the fact that in this work, for the first time, there emerges an important aspect of Michelangelo's mature style. This is the use of the nude in contorted positions to express movement, energy, and emotion. The crowded composition owes something to Bertoldo and something to Roman reliefs. Yet it is strongly Michelangelo's own. Here we can begin to sense the vigor, the power, and the tension that characterize all his later works, in whatever form or medium. He must have recognized this himself, because he kept the relief for the rest of his life.

In the spring of 1492, the year of Columbus' first voyage, there came an event that was fateful both for Florence and for Michelangelo. It happened on the night of April 8, during a fierce thunderstorm. After having suffered for some weeks from an increasingly painful illness, Lorenzo de' Medici died. He was only forty-three, and he had been so vigorous, and so life-loving a person that all Florence was shocked. His intelligence, diplomacy, imagination, and extraordinary capacity for quietly assuming responsibility had kept Florence free, prosperous, and happy for twenty-three years. On the night of his death a bolt of lightning struck the dome of the cathedral, sending heavy pieces of stone crashing into the street below in the direction of the Medici palace. And a comet, thought to be a notorious portent of disaster, streaked across the heavens. These events created a feeling of foreboding. The Florentines were fearful. They knew an era had ended, and the future looked threatening.

The Signoria hastily met and voted that Lorenzo's oldest son, Piero, should be asked to take his father's place as first citizen of the republic. Their action was understandable, since the city had prospered under the Medici for almost sixty years. But Piero, though good-natured, was arrogant and totally lacking in judgment. Three years older than Michelangelo, he had probably resented his father's attentions to the young artist. In any event, he did not invite him to continue to live in the Medici palace and go on with his work there. Michelangelo was overcome with grief. He had lost a dear friend and patron, one of the few people in his life who had understood and appreciated him. Reluctantly, he returned to the inhospitable refuge of his father's house.

The legacy of Lorenzo's friendship, however, soon enabled Michelangelo to take up his life again. The monastery of Santo Spirito had long enjoyed Medici support. For this reason, the prior invited the artist to continue his study of anatomy by dissecting corpses in the morgue of the monastery's hospital. He made this offer in spite of the fact that without official approval, such activities were then illegal and carried stiff penalties. To be able to go on with his investigations and thus gain as complete an understanding as possible of the struc-

An anonymous painting of about 1498 shows Florence's main square on the day that Savonarola was hanged and burned with two of his followers. The Palace of the Signoria is at right center; part of the Duomo can be seen at the far left.

Three small marble statuettes were carved by Michelangelo in 1494–95 for the tomb of St. Dominic, in San Dominico, Bologna.

ture and workings of the human body was a great advantage for an artist whose entire life was to be devoted to expressing his ideas, ideals, and feelings through the medium of the body.

Inspired by his study, Michelangelo sculptured a Hercules, larger than life, of which there are contemporary accounts. Purchased by a leading Florentine family, the statue was sold in later years to a king of France. After that, like so many of Michelangelo's works, it unfortunately disappeared.

Florence could not put up with Piero de' Medici for long. He was totally lacking in those qualities the Florentines so admired in his father—qualities which had led Lorenzo's fellow citizens to give him the title "the Magnificent." Piero did not respect the Florentines' fierce dedication to independence. He paraded his wealth and was proud and overbearing. This man, who came to be called Piero the Unlucky, was also ignorant beyond belief in foreign affairs, a subject in which his father, grandfather, and great grandfather had excelled.

In 1494 the formidable armies of King Charles VIII of France crossed the Alps to press his claim to

(Left) **St. Proculus**
Kneeling Angel with a Candlestick

29

the throne of Naples. France and Naples had both been allies of Florence, and Lorenzo had managed for some years to maintain a satisfactory relationship with both. Piero, however, decided to declare for Naples and named France the enemy. The French army was the best equipped in Europe. As it approached Florence, Piero fell into a panic, and abruptly changed sides. As a bribe to keep the French from sacking the city, he surrendered Florence's fortifications to them and declared Naples the enemy.

It is difficult to see how Piero could have created a worse mess. He was forced to flee and never saw Florence again. In the meantime, angry crowds plundered the Medici palace, leaving it a shell. All the wonderful collections of art, books, and manuscripts, which had been freely available to students and scholars, were dispersed. Haunted by the spirits of Cosimo, Lorenzo, and Giuliano, the building stood empty, a melancholy reminder of happier times.

The government of Florence was taken over by a fanatical monk named Savonarola. In endless sermons that were hypnotic in effect, Savonarola thundered damnation in a terrifying voice. He convinced many of the citizens that all that had happened was God's punishment for their sinfulness. He called on everyone to repent, proclaiming that the end of the world was at hand and the dreadful final judgment imminent. He declared the pope, Alexander VI, to be the Antichrist and warned that the papacy had been taken over by the forces of Satan. He instituted a strict dress code, enforcing it with wandering bands of followers armed with staves. These bands drove people off the streets with beatings and fined them on the spot if they wore attractive or fashionable articles of clothing or jewelry. In 1497, Savonarola called for all the citizens to take to the square in front of the Palace of the Signoria any paintings or statues that were not of religious subjects, as well as fine clothes, tapestries, or other rich and beautiful objects. There, they were destroyed by a great fire in what has gone down in history as the Burning of the Vanities.

Such fanaticism became too much for the Florentines, and they rose in violent reaction. In 1498, with the pope's blessing, they seized Savonarola and hanged him in the same square where the Burning of the Vanities had taken place. They burned his body in an immense bonfire. They elected a new Grand Council and the republic was restored. But all the gaiety and enjoyment of life, all the optimism and confidence of Lorenzo's time, were gone.

Before the flight of the unfortunate Piero, Michelangelo had seen the disastrous changes that were taking place. In 1494, fearing for his own safety because of his close association with the Medici, he, too, had left the city. He made his way across the Apennines and headed northeast until he reached Venice. He looked for work, but being a young stranger of nineteen without credentials, he could fine none. So he traveled south to Bologna. There, again, his good fortune came to his rescue. He was stopped at the city gates and was asked to pay an entry fee. When he said he didn't have the money, he was threatened with jail and taken before a magistrate, an aristocrat named

Gianfrancesco Aldovrandi. When the magistrate discovered that Michelangelo was a sculptor and had been a member of Lorenzo de' Medici's household, he invited him to stay at his palace.

*Raphael. **Savonarola**. 1509–10. The monk is seen at center, in profile, in this detail from a fresco in the Vatican.*

Aldovrandi assisted Michelangelo in obtaining a commission to sculpture three small statues for one of the most important works of art in the city, the elaborate tomb of St. Dominic, the founder of the Dominican order of monks. The tomb, which is in the thirteenth-century church dedicated to the saint, had been begun in 1265. Many sculptors had contributed to it. Michelangelo's statuettes, a kneeling angel with a candlestick, *St. Proculus*, and *St. Petronius*, the patron saint of Bologna, completed the monument.

Michelangelo enjoyed his stay with Aldovrandi. Life in the magistrate's palace was pleasant and comfortable, and reminded him in many ways of life with Lorenzo. He read aloud from the works of Dante and Petrarch, and there was much conversation about the arts and music. But Michelangelo became restless. After the three sculptures were finished, he felt he needed to get on with his career, and he was homesick for Florence. In the winter of 1495, as soon as he heard that order had been restored in that city, he returned, traveling on mountain roads back across the snowy Apennines.

CHAPTER IV

Fame

There was little for Michelangelo to do in a Florence still recovering from the excesses of Savonarola's rule. We know from contemporary records that at this time he carved in an antique manner a sleeping cupid, a work that has since been lost. Ascanio Condivi tells an interesting story about this statue. He recounts that, at the suggestion of Lorenzo di Pierfrancesco, a cousin of Lorenzo the Magnificent and head of the junior branch of the Medici family, Michelangelo sold the statue for thirty ducats to a dealer in art and antiquities in Rome, where there was a lively trade in such things. The dealer then sold the sculpture as an antique to a rich collector, Cardinal Raffaello Riario. He did not tell the artist the price: two hundred ducats.

After some study, the cardinal, who was something of an expert, began to suspect that the *Cupid* was not ancient, and asked for his money back. The dealer refused. So the cardinal, recognizing the extraordinary quality of the piece, decided that only a Florentine artist could have produced it. He sent a secretary to Florence to find out who the artist was. The secretary pretended to be looking for an artist to carry out certain sculptural commissions in Rome. He was soon referred to Michelangelo. He asked Michelangelo if he had ever worked in marble, and the artist mentioned a number of pieces he had carved, among them a sleeping cupid. When the cardinal's secretary explained what had happened and told him the price that Riario had paid for the "antique," Michelangelo gladly went to Rome with him to confront the crooked dealer.

The result was that the dealer reluctantly gave the cardinal back his two hundred ducats; he refused, however, to return the statue to Michelangelo for the thirty ducats he had originally paid. He argued that the piece was far too valuable to be given up for such a paltry sum. So Michelangelo didn't get his *Cupid* back, but in another lucky turn of fate, in Cardinal Riario he gained a powerful friend. Such was his introduction to Rome, where he was soon to create the first of the series of masterpieces that would earn him a unique place in the history of art.

Doni Madonna. *About 1504.*
Michelangelo painted this tondo, or round composition,
of the Holy Family to celebrate the marriage
of Agnolo Doni to Maddalena Strozzi.
(Overleaf)
This painted copy of a section of Michelangelo's lost preliminary
drawing for the fresco the Battle of Cascina was probably made
in 1542 by Aristotile da Sangallo.

Through a fellow Florentine, Michelangelo was introduced to Jacopo Galli, a Roman banker who was one of the most generous and discerning patrons of the arts of the period. Michelangelo produced two ambitious marble sculptures for Galli. These works, both of which were commissioned for Galli's formal garden, were standing male figures, larger than life and antique in subject and feeling. One, believed to have been an Apollo, was later lost. The other, a tipsy figure of Bacchus, the Roman god of wine, eventually ended up in the sculpture museum in Florence.

Galli's admiration for the two sculptures led him, Condivi tells us, to introduce Michelangelo to a friend, a French cardinal. The cardinal, who was elderly, planned soon to retire and return to France. But he wanted to leave an appropriate monument in St. Peter's, the papal cathedral in the Vatican in Rome. As a subject, he wished to commission a *pietà*. *Pietà* is the Italian word for "pity," or "mercy," but with regard to art it always refers to a specific subject, the Virgin mourning over the body of her dead Son. The subject was essentially a Northern one, common in the art of Scandinavia, Germany, and France. It was usually interpreted in a starkly expressive way, emphasizing the grisly and horrifying aspects of the theme. But Michelangelo changed all that, so that to most people the very mention of the subject has become synonymous with his unique interpretation.

On August 26, 1498, Michelangelo signed an extraordinary contract. In it he agreed to complete in marble a *pietà,* with the figure of Christ to be "of the size of a proper man, for the price of 450 golden ducats of the papal mint, . . . within one year from the day of the commencement of the work." This was followed by Jacopo Galli's pledge to the cardinal that "it shall be the finest work in marble which Rome today can show, and that no master of our days shall be able to produce a better."

It says much for Galli that he was willing to make such a pledge for an unknown young Florentine. But his trust was more than vindicated by the result. The sculpture was indeed completed within a year. Upon its installation in St. Peter's, the *Pietà* immediately became the object of admiration that has inspired countless pilgrimages from Michelangelo's time to our own day.

As specified by the contract, the body of Christ is life-size. His position, however, seems less the limpness of death than the relaxation of sleep, as if to suggest that He will rise again. The gesture of the Virgin's left hand eloquently expresses both her sorrow and her acceptance of her Son's sacrifice for the benefit of humankind. The mood is one of solemn grief and of timeless meditation on the mysteries of life and death. It is interesting to witness the effect of the *Pietà* on the many visitors who come daily from all over the world to see it. As they enter the chapel in St. Peter's where it is displayed, they fall silent. They speak, if at all, in whispers, or remain in quiet contemplation. Art such as this communicates to us across centuries of time—centuries that have seen an almost unbelievable degree of change.

Our high-tech world of instant communication is incredibly different from the world of Michelangelo. Yet we can share his sense of wonder and recognize that he created a work that, while Christian in subject, rises above divisions of religion or sect to become a meaningful symbol for all humanity.

The culminating work of Michelangelo's younger years, the *Pietà* is finished to a degree of refinement and subtlety un-matched for the time. The work is a monument to the artist's Platonic belief that ideal physical beauty is an expression of the divine. Proudly, the young sculptor, just twenty-four years of age, carved his name in Latin on the band diagonally crossing the Virgin's breast. The inscription reads: "Michelangelo Buonarroti the Florentine made it." As far as we know, the *Pietà* is the only sculpture Michelangelo ever signed. Suddenly he became the most famous sculptor in Italy.

Bacchus. 1496–97.
Michelangelo sculptured Bacchus, the god of wine of the classical world, for Jacobo Galli.

In the early spring of 1501, Michelangelo returned to Florence on hearing from a friend that the Board of Works of the cathedral was considering giving him a commission for a major sculpture. For years an immense block of marble had been stored in the workyard of the cathedral. Approximately rectangular, it was just under twenty feet high and weighed tons. A generation earlier, a sculptor had started roughing out the block but had abandoned the project in dismay at the chunk's colossal size. Michelangelo had known about "the Giant," as it was familiarly called, since the time he had worked with Bertoldo in the Medici Gardens of San Marco many years before.

There had been several suggestions made by various sculptors over the years as to possible uses for the block, but the board had rejected them all. Now Michelangelo was offered the Giant. The commission was not only a challenge but an honor. A contract was drawn up with the board and the Wool Merchants' Guild that guaranteed Michelangelo an income for two years while he carried out the work. He proposed to carve a huge figure of David, the biblical hero. The idea met with universal approval.

Bruges Madonna. 1501–4. Done for a Flemish merchant family, this sculpture shows the Virgin as grave and thoughtful, like the Virgin of Michelangelo's Pietà of 1498–99.

Pietà. 1498–99. St. Peter's, Rome. The Pietà stands in its own chapel in St. Peter's. In 1972 an insane man attacked it with a hammer, damaging the Virgin's face. All the fragments were saved, and the work has been beautifully restored by Vatican conservators.

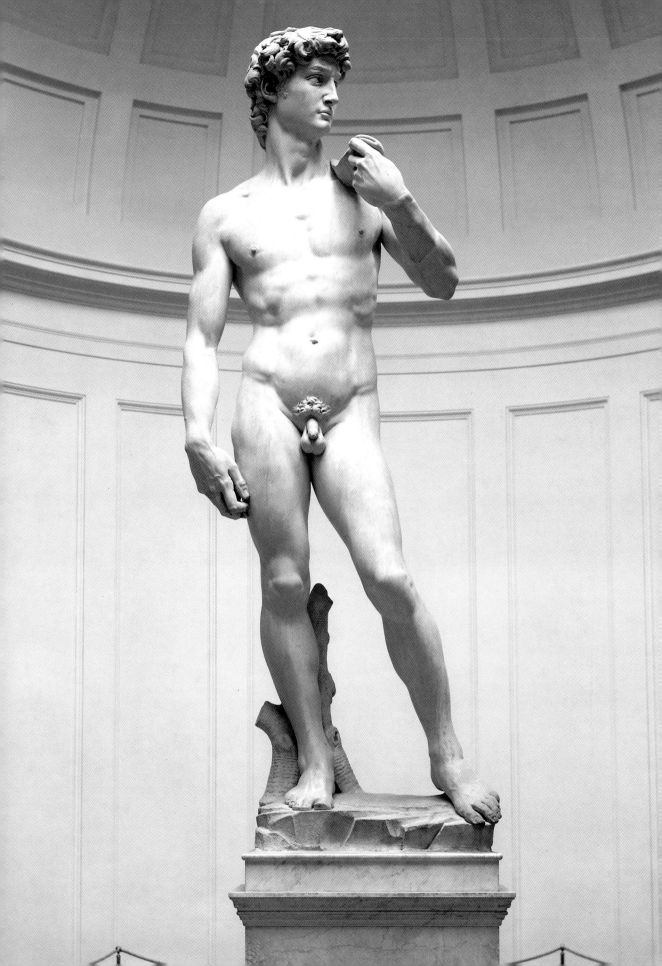

There was a special reason why the idea was popular. The republic of Florence was a small state surrounded by larger and more powerful ones. Yet the Florentines had managed through wise leadership and superior diplomacy to retain those rights won by their ancestors from their feudal overlords many years earlier. Almost all the other states in Italy were despotically ruled. Many times over the years, through treachery or by attempted conquest, Florence had been threatened by would-be tyrants, both from within and without, but had managed with courage and determination to remain free. So David, the youth who had slain the giant enemy, Goliath, was felt to be an appropriate symbol of the spirit of the city.

As the sun rose on September 13, 1501, Michelangelo had already begun work on his monumental sculpture. He worked in a large timber shelter that the crew of the cathedral had constructed around the huge marble block. To enable him to reach all parts of the block, a scaffold had been built that could be adjusted in height and position. Armed with the traditional tools of the stonecutter—hammers, chisels, rasps, and files—he attacked the marble. Steadily, the chips piled up around the base of the block as he worked through the long days of summer, and, by torchlight, during the short days of winter. Gradually, as he labored tirelessly, the gigantic figure emerged from the stone. Finally, after two and a half years, the statue was completed. It was padded and roped in a cagelike framework of heavy timbers mounted upon rollers. Over a period of several days it was moved, with the help of many expert workmen, to the position Michelangelo had chosen for it in front of the Palace of the Signoria.

Early in September 1504, the *David* was revealed with appropriate ceremony to the crowds of admiring citizens that filled the square. For them then, as for us today, it symbolized courage, justice, and good government as expressed through Michelangelo's Platonic vision of the ideal youthful hero and ruler. Vigilant and valiant, the *David* expresses the awesome power that the Italians call *terribilità*.

*David. 1501–4. Originally placed in front
of the Palace of the Signoria, David was moved indoors in 1873
to save it from further weathering. A copy was put in
its place in the piazza.*

Everyone was profoundly impressed by the *David*. The Signoria immediately engaged Michelangelo to sculpture the twelve apostles for the cathedral. These figures were to be delivered at the rate of one a year, and he was to receive a steady income during the twelve years. During this period he was to live in a house nearby that was to become his own property when the series was complete. Despite the fact that he had just made a commitment to carve twelve gigantic figures in twelve years, Michelangelo had scarcely finished the *David* when he decided to undertake yet another major project. He agreed to the challenge of the painting of a fresco for the Grand Council's hall in the Palace of the Signoria.

Leonardo da Vinci had already begun work on the preliminary drawing for a companion mural on the opposite wall of the immense interior. Recently returned from Milan, Leonardo had earned a reputation as the leading artist of his time. His famous painting the *Last Supper* and his tremendous, more than life-size clay model, known as "the Great Horse," for an equestrian monument for the duke of Milan, had won him fame throughout Europe. Leonardo was twenty-three years older than Michelangelo. But the differences between the two men lay in more than their ages. Leonardo seemed, in everything except

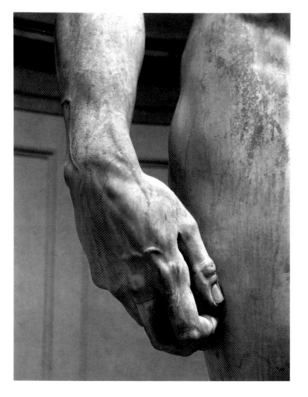

artistic genius, Michelangelo's opposite. Where Michelangelo was touchy and standoffish, Leonardo was always courteous and approachable. Where Michelangelo was awkward in company, Leonardo was always at ease, a perfect courtier and diplomat. His knowledge was encyclopedic, his interests incredibly wide and varied, and his achievements legendary. Emboldened by the great success of the *David*, Michelangelo's fierce pride drove him to pit himself against the older master.

Leonardo was assigned the subject of the Battle of Anghiari, a cavalry engagement that would enable him, as the greatest expert in anatomy of the age, to put to use his masterful skill in rendering both men and horses. Michelangelo prepared to paint the Battle of Cascina, a skirmish in which Florentine troops were surprised by English forces while taking a cooling swim in the Arno River, but were nevertheless able to rally and vanquish the enemy. It was a perfect choice for Michelangelo because it gave him the opportunity to depict his favorite subject, the heroic nude in action.

Both artists completed full-scale preliminary drawings of their subjects which were much admired. The art-loving Florentines regarded the affair as a battle of giants. Because both artists were Florentine, the city would be the winner, gaining two great works by the two greatest artists of the time. But through a curious twist of fate, neither of these potentially superb works of art was ever completed. Leonardo had scarcely begun before the French government of Milan demanded of the reluctant Signoria that he immediately return to that city. A greater force still was abruptly to change all of Michelangelo's and the Signoria's plans for his future. Shortly after New Year's Day in 1505, Pope Julius II summoned him to Rome.

Though neither of the two murals was finished, they were two of the most influential works of the period. The full-scale and other drawings for them were studied by artists from all over Europe and they became a veritable art school for succeeding generations. For more than a century after the execution of the drawings, forms, details, and gestures taken from them appeared in paintings, sculptures, drawings, and prints from all parts of Europe. Over the years the drawings were treasured like holy relics—literally studied to pieces until only fragments remained. Today nothing whatsoever is left of them, but their influence on the development of Western art is incalculable.

Raphael. **Pope Julius II.** *1512. This detail from a fresco in the Vatican captures the forceful spirit of the warrior pope who was Michelangelo's greatest and most demanding patron.*

CHAPTER V

Julius, the Warrior Pope

In 1503 Cardinal Giuliano della Rovere became Pope Julius II. He was a formidable warrior who loved life in the field and on the march. But he also had visions of grandeur to match Michelangelo's own. He resolved to restore the papacy, which had been weakened by years of misrule, scandalous divisions, and the diversion of church funds into private pockets. He determined to rebuild ramshackle Rome into an ideal capital for a renewed world church. He had the physique and stamina of a linebacker and the tolerance of a drill sergeant, but he was cultured, highly intelligent, idealistic, and had a passion for the arts. Everything Julius did was done with immense energy. Astride his great war horse, clad in polished steel armor, with his beard streaming in the wind, he personally led the papal armies in the field, urging them on like some crusader king of the Middle Ages attacking the infidel. Just as tirelessly, he amassed antiquities, laying the foundation for the present Vatican holdings, among the finest in the world. With equal vigor he went about the rebuilding of Rome. His aim was to restore it to a magnificence to match the splendor of the city to which all roads led in the great days of the ancient empire.

Giuliano da Sangallo, a fellow Florentine and friend of Michelangelo's, was the papal architect and consultant to the pope on matters concerning the arts. It was he who urged Julius to enlist Michelangelo's services. Throughout his reign, Julius was to be Michelangelo's greatest patron and admirer. But he also caused the artist much pain and trouble because of his constant demands, arbitrary decisions, and, above all, his hair-trigger temper.

During the fourteenth century the papacy had fallen on hard times. In 1309 the pope retreated from Rome to Avignon in France, and the city of Rome declined. There were no more activities of the papal court, with streams of foreign visitors and embassies from distant kingdoms, no more throngs of devout pilgrims. The papal states had previously extended from Ferrara and Bologna in the north, continuing east of Florence through Urbino and Perugia, and south to the borders of the kingdom of Naples. With the pope far away in France, the papal states fell apart. They were taken over by ambitious soldiers of fortune or local lords.

The ancient city of Rome itself shrank to a fraction of its former size. Within its centuries-old walls there were acres and acres of wasteland—fragments of crumbling ruins overgrown with vegetation amid farms and vineyards. Cattle, sheep, and goats roamed over what had been the forum, in the center of old Rome, grazing among the fallen columns and broken remnants of masonry. Churches and palaces were falling down. The city was infested with roving bands of brigands and was the scene of constant struggles for control among warring lords. Noble temples, baths, and other public buildings became quarries for the stone which was used to transform a few of them into fortified strongholds for the feuding barons.

When in 1417 Martin V was elected pope by a church council, he succeeded in eliminating rivals and consolidating his position. On his arrival in Rome in 1420, he set about to restore law and order and rebuild the city. He also began to restore the Church to a position of strength and respectability. He was the first of a series of strong-minded, vigorous, and warlike popes leading up to the redoubtable Julius II.

By the time of Julius's succession in 1503, then, there had been seventy-five years of effort to repair the damage of centuries. Much had been accomplished, but far more needed to be done, and Julius was determined to do it. He was elected at the age of sixty, so he felt the pressure of time. The force of his personality and the size of his ambitions were such that, armed with absolute power, he was bound to stir up a storm. Inevitably, Michelangelo would be

Ceiling of the Sistine Chapel. 1508–12. Michelangelo's fresco illustrates scenes from the biblical account in the book of Genesis of the creation of the world and of humankind. He also included the ancestors of Christ and the Old Testament prophets and classical sibyls who foretold Christ's coming. Working alone, Michelangelo completed the huge ceiling in less than four and a half years, perhaps the greatest accomplishment of any artist in history.

(Above) **Study for the Libyan Sibyl on the Sistine Ceiling. 1511**
(Right) **Study for the head of Leda. 1529–30**

caught up in the resulting tempest.

For centuries, the ancient papal cathedral of St. Peter's had been falling into increasing disrepair. Dedicated in the year 326 by Pope Sylvester during the reign of Constantine the Great, the first Christian emperor of Rome, it had been the head church of Christendom for almost 1,200 years. With a ground plan longer than a football field, it was conceived on a truly imperial scale. But Julius wanted to rebuild it in an even grander form. He asked Giuliano da Sangallo and a comparative newcomer to papal service, the architect Donato Bramante, to draw up plans. Both of the submitted concepts were indeed grand, but the pope preferred Bramante's. Sangallo, who had been a loyal friend and follower of the pope, was deeply hurt by the rejection.

Meanwhile, Julius had already put Michelangelo to work on a special project for the new cathedral—the pope's own tomb, to be constructed under the dome of the cathedral. It was planned on a scale impressive enough to suit Julius's ambitions.

In the early days of the project, Julius made constant visits to Michelangelo's studio to inspect his progress. But as the pope became increasingly eager to get on with the construction of the new St. Peter's, his visits became less frequent. Finally, during Holy Week in 1506, he ordered that the work on the tomb be suspended.

Both Michelangelo and Sangallo thought, probably quite correctly, that the pope's behavior was influenced by Bramante, who, to safeguard his own future, was trying to undermine their positions with Julius. Michelangelo tried to see Julius but was refused an audience. He reacted with his usual impetuosity, immediately taking off for Florence. Julius sent a horseman after him with an angry ultimatum. But the messenger wasn't able to catch up with the artist until after he had crossed the border into Florentine territory. Michelangelo issued his own ultimatum: he would not return until

Julius paid him what he owed him and promised to abide by his agreements.

Julius was livid with rage. He bombarded the Signoria with a series of threatening messages commanding that Michelangelo be returned to Rome, by force if necessary. Finally, as Condivi records, the leader of the Signoria, who was an old friend of Michelangelo's, told him, "We do not wish to have to go to war on your account," and advised him to go back.

After months of diplomatic skirmishing, the matter was finally resolved in the summer of 1506. At that time the pope took to the warpath to punish and bring back into the papal fold the tyrants of Perugia and Bologna. Personally leading a force of hundreds of knights and a battalion of specially trained assault troops, the original of today's Swiss Guard, he cowed the two despots into surrendering. He then sent a message to Michelangelo, commanding his presence in Bologna. Under the protection of a document naming him an official ambassador of the Florentine republic, Michelangelo complied. After the pope had vented his wrath on an attendant bishop or two, the pair settled their differences. Soon after this, Julius ordered Michelangelo to sculpture a ten-foot-high bronze statue of himself enthroned. This papal portrait statue was to be mounted high on the facade of Bologna's cathedral to remind the citizens who was boss.

In the spring of 1508 there occurred another event behind which the influence of Bramante could be subtly detected. Julius called Michelangelo to Rome to execute another of his favorite projects, the painting of the ceiling of the Sistine Chapel in the Vatican. Both Condivi and Michelangelo suspected that Bramante, to strengthen his position in the pope's favor and continue as architect of St. Peter's, had persuaded Julius to make the assignment. The painting would keep Michelangelo from returning to his work on the pope's tomb and would involve him in something he didn't want to do. Therefore it might bog him down in time-consuming difficulties. It might even yield less than satisfactory results, thus discrediting Michelangelo in the pope's eyes.

Michelangelo, in fact, did not want the project. He protested that he was not a painter but a sculptor. He strongly recommended a promising young painter, then twenty-five, named Raffaello Sanzio (known to history as Raphael), who was then decorating the walls of a series of rooms in the papal palace. But the pope was adamant. After much papal scolding, Michelangelo gave in. He started the work on May 10, 1508. He was thirty-three years old, and he bitterly resented the project he was being forced to undertake.

Twenty years earlier, while working in Ghirlandaio's shop, Michelangelo

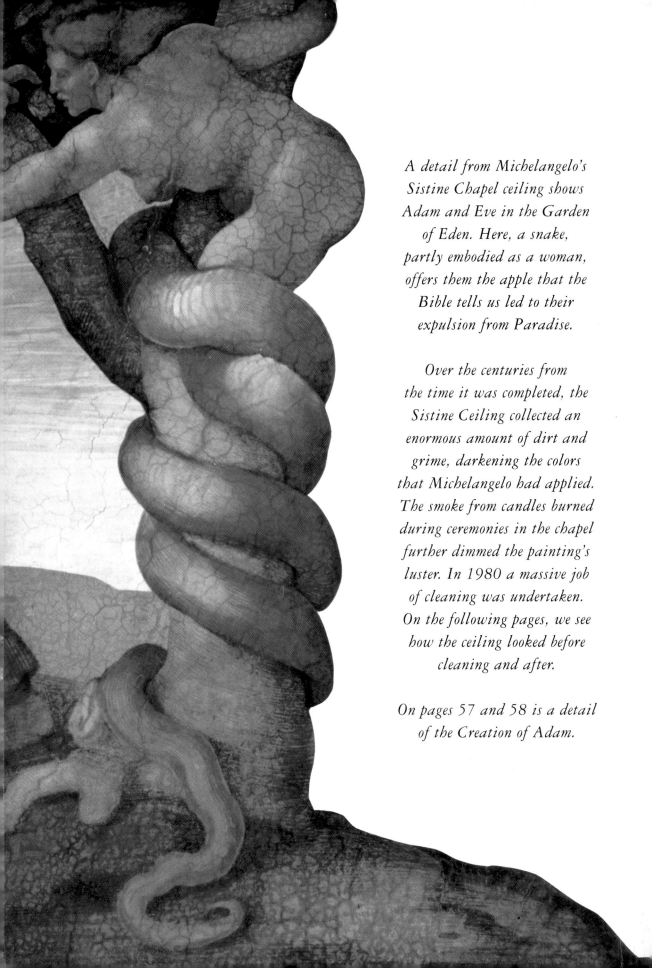

A detail from Michelangelo's
Sistine Chapel ceiling shows
Adam and Eve in the Garden
of Eden. Here, a snake,
partly embodied as a woman,
offers them the apple that the
Bible tells us led to their
expulsion from Paradise.

Over the centuries from
the time it was completed, the
Sistine Ceiling collected an
enormous amount of dirt and
grime, darkening the colors
that Michelangelo had applied.
The smoke from candles burned
during ceremonies in the chapel
further dimmed the painting's
luster. In 1980 a massive job
of cleaning was undertaken.
On the following pages, we see
how the ceiling looked before
cleaning and after.

On pages 57 and 58 is a detail
of the Creation of Adam.

had received an excellent grounding in fresco painting. This is the technique of painting on freshly applied wet plaster so that as the plaster and the paint dry together, the painting becomes an integral part of the wall. It is a monumental method because it is so permanent. But working on wet plaster is tricky. Each day just enough new plaster has to be applied so that the artist can paint it in one day. If the plaster is allowed to dry, the paint will not be absorbed and become one with the wall.

Because he had not painted in fresco for twenty years, Michelangelo asked for assistants from Florence. He soon found, however, that they did not live up to his demanding standards, so he dismissed them and decided to do the entire vault himself. The vault's surface covered 5,800 square feet—larger than the entire playing area of a tennis court—and its curved shape made the work still more difficult. It was a superhuman task, and it is doubtful that any other artist known could have accomplished it.

Michelangelo worked on a scaffold some fifty feet above the pavement. In order to paint, he had to stand partly crouching, with his back "bent as bowmen bend a bow in Spain," as he wrote in a famous poem describing his efforts. "My beard points to heaven, . . . my paintbrush all the day does drop a rich mosaic on my face."

Julius came almost daily to watch the progress of the gigantic work, always urging Michelangelo to hurry. Finally, in the fall of 1512, Condivi tells us, the pope impatiently demanded again when he would finish. Michelangelo answered as usual, "When I can." "When I can!" the pope shouted angrily, and struck him with his cane.

Michelangelo climbed down from the scaffold and prepared to leave for Florence. A papal secretary hurried after him to convey the pope's apologies, and he was persuaded to return to work. But the next day the pope roared at him again and threatened to have him thrown from the scaffold. So, reluctantly, Michelangelo had the scaffold removed, leaving the ceiling without the few finishing touches that he had planned to apply to complete it to his satisfaction. On the last day of October in 1512 the ceiling was shown, first to the inhabitants of the Vatican, and then to throngs of the public. As a result, Michelangelo was recognized not only as the greatest sculptor, but also as the greatest painter of his time.

Four months later, the pope, seventy years of age, died. Perhaps he drove Michelangelo so hard because he sensed that he did not have long to live and desperately wanted to see the ceiling finished.

CHAPTER VI

Times of Terror

The demanding presence of Julius was gone. But what Condivi called "the tragedy of the tomb," the contract binding Michelangelo to complete the pope's funeral monument, still remained. On Julius's death in 1513, his executors signed a new contract with Michelangelo, and he returned to the project, working on it steadily for the next three years.

The original design for the Julius tomb planned for St. Peter's was for a freestanding structure, like a memorial chapel, with forty marble statues as well as other carved decorations. Over time the concept changed—the freestanding structure became a wall tomb, and it was decided to shift its location from St. Peter's to the Roman church that had been assigned to Julius when he was elevated to cardinal. The church has the curious name of San Pietro in Vincoli, St. Peter in Chains, because the chains with which it was believed St. Peter was shackled in prison are preserved there.

Michelangelo was to continue work on the tomb until 1545. At that time, at the age of seventy, having worked on the tomb intermittently for forty years, he was finally released from his contract.

The final form of the monument is much reduced, and a number of figures made to meet earlier designs for it ended up elsewhere. Though greatly diminished in size from the original conception, the tomb is still strikingly impressive, especially because of its centerpiece, the unforgettable figure of the Old Testament prophet Moses. Considerably larger than life, the figure was sculptured during the years 1513–16, when Michelangelo was able to devote all his time to the tomb project. The Moses has been interpreted as being a spiritual portrait of Julius or of Michelangelo himself. Probably it is something

The tomb of Pope Julius II was completed in 1545 in the church of
San Pietro in Vincoli in Rome.

of both, embodying the grand visions which were pursued with such passion by both men. Both also shared that quality of power and immense vitality, so dramatically expressed in the *Moses*, summed up in the word the Italians always associate with Michelangelo, *terribilità*.

The *Moses* probably derived from the bronze of Julius that Michelangelo had made for the cathedral of Bologna. The prophet clutches the tablets brought down from Mount Sinai, according to the biblical account. He glares wrathfully at a sinful world sorely in need of God's law, inscribed on the tablets. The curious horns, which appear in many older likenesses of the prophet, are the result of an error in the Latin Vulgate Bible. The Old Testament describes Moses as having rays of light radiating from his brow. The Hebrew word for light was mistakenly translated in the Vulgate as "horns." Because of Michelangelo's long and troubled struggle with the Julius tomb, the *Moses* has come to be seen as a monument not only to the pope, but to the sculptor as well.

Just as Florence, because of the enlightened patronage of the Medici, had become during the fifteenth century the center of the Early Renaissance, Rome, through the enthusiasm of Julius and his successors, became the center of the High Renaissance during the following century. On Julius's death in 1513, Michelangelo's boyhood companion Giovanni de' Medici, son of Lorenzo the Magnificent, was elected pope as Leo X. Leo shared his father's interests, and attracted a brilliant circle of artists, scholars, musicians, and writers to his court. In the winter of 1521, after a reign of eight years, Leo died suddenly of malaria. Because of the vast sums he had spent on the construction of St. Peter's and on the acquisition of works of art, manuscripts, and antiquities for the Vatican collection, his death left the papacy tremendously in debt.

In 1523, another Medici, Giulio, son of Lorenzo the Magnificent's brother Giuliano, and also a boyhood friend of Michelangelo, became pope as Clement VII. The reigns of the Medici popes were times of great strife. The papacy was involved in a confusion of wars and constantly shifting alliances, as the kings of France and the Holy Roman Emperor contended for control of Italy and, indeed, of Europe. A low point was reached when, in 1527, Rome, the very capital of Christendom, was captured by the forces of Charles V, the Holy Roman Emperor. With an army made up mostly of Spanish renegades and German mercenaries, the captors sacked the city with an unbelievable ferocity. Clement VII retreated to the fortress of the Castel Sant'Angelo, which he eventually had to surrender to the imperial forces. In the meantime, the looting, torture, slaughter, and burning went on for weeks.

Michelangelo was in Florence at the time, working on the New Sacristy of the Medici church of San Lorenzo. The project had been commissioned in 1519 by Pope Leo X as a funerary chapel for the Medici family: The Old Sacristy had been designed, almost exactly a century earlier, by the great Early Renaissance architect, Brunelleschi, who had also designed and built the superb dome of the city's cathedral. Michelangelo planned the New Sacristy with an almost identical exterior and ground plan to the old one. The two interiors, however, are entirely different. Where Brunelleschi's is shadowed, Michelangelo's is flooded with light which falls from the four windows in the base of the dome and from the oculus, the round opening at its peak. The interior rises dramatically from the inlaid marble pavement through four stages to the oculus. The walls are plain plaster. The architectural members are of the beautiful grayish stone beloved of the Florentines and appropriately called *pietra serena*, "serene stone." The sculptures are in white marble. Although the two Medici popes intended the chapel to include the tombs of their fathers, Lorenzo the Magnificent and his brother Giuliano, the only monuments ultimately carried out were those to two lesser-known members of the family, Giuliano, duke of Nemours, and Lorenzo, duke of Urbino. Both had served as captains in the papal army and had died as young men.

The idea of the chapel is a fusion of Christian and Platonic ideals. The statues of the two dukes are not portraits. As Michelangelo remarked, no one would care

Moses. About 1513–16. Michelangelo had sculptured the Moses for an earlier, larger version of the tomb of Pope Julius II.

63

*Medici Chapel, San Lorenzo, Florence. 1519–34. At right is the tomb of
Lorenzo, duke of Urbino. On the duke's sarcophagus are male and female
figures representing Dusk and Dawn. Flanking the Madonna at left are saints
Cosmas and Damian, the Medici patron saints, executed by Michelangelo's
pupils to his design. In the sarcophagus-base for the three sculptures, Lorenzo
the Magnificent and his brother, Giuliano, are buried.*

what they looked like a thousand years later. The figures were intended not as
likenesses, but rather as symbols of the souls of the departed captains. Both
look toward the sculpture of the Madonna and Child at the end of the chapel,
contemplating the supreme truth that the group symbolizes. The powerful,
sorrowing figures of Night and Day, and of Dawn and Dusk, recline on the
caskets below the seated dukes. They suggest the passage of time, which, as

Michelangelo wrote, "consumes all things," and the restless change that characterizes our world in contrast to the timelessness of eternity, where the souls of the dead have found permanent refuge.

Other sculptures were to have been added to complete Michelangelo's grand scheme for the chapel. But fate intervened in the form of a particularly unpleasant youth, a bastard of the Medici family named Alessandro. In 1532, Alessandro had been forcibly installed as duke of Florence by Pope Clement VII, with the help of an army. No one knew for sure who his parents were, though it was widely rumored that they were the pope himself and a Moorish slave. The young man's dark color and tightly curled hair made the rumor seem believable, but nothing could explain his violent, irrational, and murderous nature. For some reason he had developed an intense hatred of Michelangelo. The artist was understandably afraid of him, and with reason feared assassination, either by the duke himself or by the brutish gang with which he surrounded himself. Michelangelo's only protection was the continuing support and friendship of the pope. So when in the early summer of 1534 he received word that Clement's health was failing, he quietly left Florence for the safety of Rome. He arrived on September 23; two days later, the pope was dead. Again Michelangelo's good fortune had saved him.

Clement was succeeded by Cardinal Alessandro Farnese as Paul III. A friend and admirer of Michelangelo and another of the great patrons of the arts, Paul, too, favored writers, artists, and scholars. As in Leo's time, the papal

Madonna and Child.
Medici Chapel.

court was the scene of masked balls, banquets, and musical performances. Paul rebuilt and repaired the dreadful damages suffered during the Sack of Rome by the imperial armies seven years before. He also added to the Vatican's collections of art and antiquities.

In 1534, Paul asked Michelangelo to undertake another enormous task in the Sistine Chapel: to paint the *Last Judgment* on the altar wall. Michelangelo's immense fresco measures forty-eight by forty-four feet. Again, he carried it out alone, and it took him five and a half years (1536–41) to complete.

The subject is a terrifying one, the final fate meted out to souls for all eternity. Yet it seems all the more overwhelming because of Michelangelo's interpretation of it. He was now over sixty, and during the twenty-four years that had intervened between the painting of the ceiling and the wall, the optimistic Renaissance world had been shattered. Violence was everywhere. Rome itself had suffered the unthinkable humiliation of capture and devastation. Outbursts of the plague had killed millions across Europe. The Western world was divided by the Protestant Reformation, which had split the church and had led, as religious conflicts seem always to do, to bloody crusades, burnings at the stake, and endless human suffering. Michelangelo felt the weight of his years, and approached the task with determination but with a sense that the world faced a gloomy destiny.

In the upper center, a muscular and beardless Christ, with the Virgin seated by His side, stands in judgment, surrounded by crowds of figures full of restless energy. With upraised hand, He pronounces the fateful decree on the many souls that rise from their graves below, either to mount upward, aided by

(Right)
The tomb of
Giuliano de Medici
with figures repre-
senting Night (at
left) and Day.

angelic spirits, or to descend, dragged down by demons. At the bottom, the ghastly figure of Charon, brandishing an oar, ferries the damned across the dark waters of the river Styx toward the gaping mouth of hell. Grouped around Christ are a host of saints, many of whom carry the symbols of their martyrdom. Below Christ is a group of angels blowing their horns to wake the dead from their prolonged sleep. Every figure in the immense and crowded composition is in motion, in poses and with gestures of the greatest variety and inventiveness. The result is tremendously dynamic and dramatic. So overwhelming is the impact of the immense work, that, when it was unveiled on October 31, 1541, and Paul III finally saw it complete and unobstructed by scaffolding, he fell to his knees in awe.

In keeping with the Platonic idea of the human body as "the visible aspect of the soul," Michelangelo represented the *Last Judgment* figures in the nude. During the reigns of Julius II and Leo X, few, if any, would have questioned the propriety of this, so generally accepted was the Platonic ideal. By the time of Paul III, however, the more puritanical spirit of the Reformation had come to be felt, even in papal circles. Biagio da Cesena, an important official in the papal court, objected to the nudity as more appropriate to a bar than to a church. Michelangelo responded by painting into his fresco a portrait of Biagio in the depths of hell, with horns, and clad only in the coils of a serpent. Biagio protested to the pope, who was highly amused and considered the portrait a fitting and witty response to Biagio's carping. Some years later, however, when the spirit of reform had reached its height, another pope, Paul IV, again brought up the matter of nudity. As Vasari tells us, Michelangelo good-naturedly replied that reforming the painting was no great matter, and that "His Holiness need not concern himself with that, but should look to continuing to set the world in order." As a result, one of the artist's assistants, thereafter known to the Romans as "Daniel the breeches-maker," was commissioned to paint draperies over the offending details.

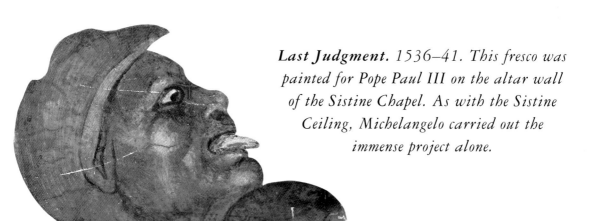

Last Judgment. 1536–41. *This fresco was painted for Pope Paul III on the altar wall of the Sistine Chapel. As with the Sistine Ceiling, Michelangelo carried out the immense project alone.*

CHAPTER VII

Times of Triumph

During the years when he was working on the *Last Judgment*, Michelangelo developed two of the closest friendships of his life. One was with the young and brilliant Roman aristocrat Tommaso dei Cavalieri, and the other was with Vittoria Colonna, a noble lady of an old and distinguished Roman family. Both individuals were dedicated to reforming the church from within, and both had strong intellectual and artistic interests. Vittoria was famous for her mystical religious poetry, which was widely known and admired. Though she had castles, palaces, and great estates, she lived mostly in convents, leading a contemplative life. She enjoyed frequent gatherings of friends with similar interests, and these meetings often included Michelangelo. They carried on lively discussions about literature and the arts.

To these two friends, Tommaso and Vittoria, Michelangelo, probably for the first time since leaving the household of Lorenzo the Magnificent, opened his heart. Both valued and admired him, not only for his tremendous creative power but also as a unique and heroic individual. The many letters and poems Michelangelo exchanged with them express shared ideals and also reflect a shift in emphasis in Michelangelo's thinking. He was especially influenced by the clarity and strength of Vittoria's religious faith. Christian ideals began increasingly to prevail over the Platonic ideas in his philosophy.

About the time Michelangelo completed the *Last Judgment*, he carved a symbolic bust of Brutus, the Roman statesman who had assassinated Julius Caesar in 44 B.C. to prevent the Roman republic from falling under the sway of a dictator. During the Renaissance, Brutus came to stand for all public-spirited

Brutus. This bust was carved about 1540 to commemorate the assassination of Duke Alessandro de' Medici, freeing Florence from his despotic rule. The Roman Brutus was considered a hero for killing a tyrant.

citizens, who, by the murder of a tyrant, maintain their country's freedom. The portrait bust, carried out in the manner of a Roman sculpture of ancient times, is Michelangelo's celebration of the deliverance of Florence from the brutal tyranny of Alessandro, murdered in 1537 by Lorenzino de' Medici, of the junior branch of the family. Like all Florentines, Michelangelo was intensely relieved by the removal of the hated Moor, who had already poisoned his cousin, Cardinal Ippolito de' Medici, the only other male in the main line. It has been suggested that the bust is an idealized portrait of Lorenzino, who was the legitimate heir to the duchy. Lorenzino, however, fearing the revenge of Alessandro's cutthroat companions, had not claimed the duchy but had instead fled to Venice, leaving the succession to his seventeen-year-old cousin Cosimo.

Cosimo de' Medici was a handsome, polite, and personable young

The entrance hall and staircase of the Laurentian Library, San Lorenzo, Florence. The library was begun by Michelangelo in 1524. His design for the hall and staircase was carried out by the architect Ammanati in 1560.

man. To everyone's amazement, he turned out to be a vigorous and demanding ruler of considerable ability. He managed in 1555 to annex the neighboring republic of Siena and by 1569 had transformed the Dukedom of Florence into the Grand Duchy of Tuscany, which remained under Medici rule until 1737, when the Medici line died out.

Cosimo was a serious and knowing patron of the arts. He was eager to have Michelangelo return to Florence to complete the Medici tombs in the New Sacristy and to finish the Laurentian Library above the cloisters of San Lorenzo. Over a period of several years he sent frequent letters and messengers to Rome, urging Michelangelo to resume work on the projects. When it became clear that Michelangelo was not only aging, but was also totally preoccupied with St. Peter's, Cosimo asked him to send his plans for the Florence projects so that other artists could complete them. Michelangelo replied sadly that the plans existed only in his mind. But he eventually sent a model for the grand staircase of the Laurentian Library. Its curious, curving stair treads and the pairs of columns embedded in the walls made it a strikingly

Conversion of St. Paul.
1542–45. The detail above from the fresco at right at the Vatican, Rome, shows Saul the Pharisee on the road to Damascus after blinding light coming from the heavenly figure of Jesus brought a revelation so shattering that he fell from his horse. As a result, he became the Apostle Paul, the devoted follower of Christ.

original design. When the stair hall was finally finished about 1560, it provided a dramatic introduction to the classically peaceful interior of the long library, a treasure house of illuminated manuscripts and rare books collected by several generations of the Medici family.

In 1542 Paul III commissioned two more frescoes from Michelangelo, the *Conversion of St. Paul* and the *Martyrdom of St. Peter*. They were to occupy the central sections of facing walls in the pope's chapel in the Vatican, which had just recently been completed. Though the frescoes are far smaller than those in the Sistine Chapel, they were enough by this time to tax even Michelangelo. The sheer physical labor of working against time to paint on the wet plaster which had to be applied daily, and doing this while perched on a scaffolding, often having to assume awkward and tiring positions, was tremendous. As Michelangelo wrote Vasari, "Painting . . . in fresco is not for old men."

By 1550, when the frescoes were completed, Michelangelo was seventy-five years old. Vittoria Colonna had died three years earlier. Her death was a terrible blow to him, and he felt a painful loss. At about this time he started

work on a Deposition, a sculpture showing Christ's body after having been lowered from the cross. The composition of this piece follows closely a drawing he made for Vittoria. The limp body is being supported by Mary Magdalene and the Virgin. A sorrowing Joseph of Arimathea, a devoted follower of Jesus who offered his own family's rock-cut tomb for His burial, stands compassionately behind. The figure of Mary Magdalene was later reworked by another sculptor. But Michelangelo made the face of Joseph a self-portrait, an indication that he intended the group to be his own grave monument. The sculpture was never used for that purpose, however; it was Vasari who designed Michelangelo's memorial in Santa Croce. The *Deposition* is now in the cathedral of Florence, beneath Brunelleschi's magnificent dome that Michelangelo so admired.

In the autumn of 1547, Pope Paul had appointed Michelangelo architect of St. Peter's. Though work on the cathedral had been going on for forty years or so, it had gone slowly. So Michelangelo was free to make whatever changes he thought necessary. Above all he wanted a monumental simplicity even greater than that of Bramante's original plan. So the first thing he did was to scrap the designs of his immediate predecessor, Antonio da Sangallo.

There were many in the Vatican, however, who had admired Sangallo's fussier and far more ornate design. These people objected loudly to the change, protested to the pope, and circulated scandalous stories about Michelangelo. The pope eventually responded with a papal brief—an official statement of church policy—that effectively blasted the opposition. "Forasmuch," it began, "as our beloved son,

Michelangelo's second fresco (1545–50) for the Pauline Chapel portrays the crucifixion of St. Peter. Peter asked to be crucified upside-down out of respect for the manner of Christ's suffering and death.

76

Michelangelo Buonarroti, a Florentine citizen, a member of our household, and our regular dining companion, has remade . . . in a better shape, a . . . plan of the fabric of the Basilica of the Prince of the Apostles in Rome, . . . we hereby approve and confirm the aforementioned new design." The brief went on to appoint Michelangelo "for as long as he shall live, . . . with the authority to change, refashion, enlarge and contract" the building "as shall seem best to him . . . without seeking permission . . . from anyone else whatsoever." It was a ringing affirmation of the pope's trust, and for the moment all seemed well. But within weeks Paul was stricken with a fever and suddenly died.

Again Michelangelo's enemies, as Vasari tells us, sought to oust him. They persuaded the new pope, Julius III, to call a meeting in the unfinished church. The gathering included Roman noblemen, prominent churchmen, Vatican officials, leading citizens, and Michelangelo with his foremen and workmen. During the meeting, an influential and admired cardinal, Marcello Cervini, the head of the Vatican Library, reproached Michelangelo with not having planned for enough light for the building's interior. Michelangelo explained that there were to be windows in the vaulting. "But you never told us anything about that," the cardinal complained. "I am not obliged to tell your lordship or anyone else what I do or intend to do," Michelangelo answered. "Your business is to provide the money and see that it is not stolen. The building is my affair."

The pope was so delighted at Michelangelo's spirit that he invited the artist to visit his private villa, where the two had lengthy and pleasant

Deposition.
About 1550–55. Michelangelo never completely finished this work, which he intended for his own tomb. In 1721 the group was placed in the cathedral in Florence.

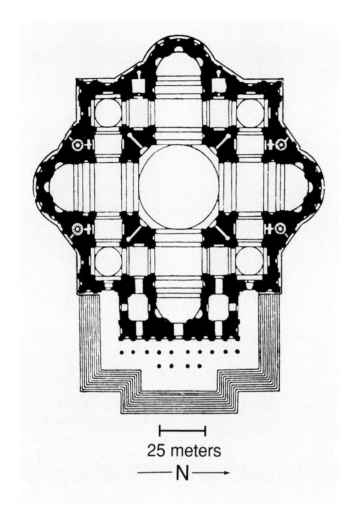

*Michelangelo's ground
plan for St. Peter's
in the Vatican shows
the clarity and simplicity
of his interpretation
of Bramante's
original concept. The
columned portico indicated
here by dots was extended
after Michelangelo's death
into the tremendous nave
that exists today.*

25 meters

N →

discussions about art and architecture. Succeeding popes confirmed Michelangelo's authority, and the work on St. Peter's went on apace according to his own unique vision.

In the meantime Michelangelo had also been working on another of Pope Paul's commissions, the redesigning and rebuilding of the old Roman imperial Capitol. Since the days of the ancient republic, the Capitol had been the historic center not only of the city, but also of the Western world. It was built on the hill known as the Capitoline, highest of the legendary seven hills of ancient Rome. As the result of years of neglect, it had fallen into shabby disrepair.

In Michelangelo's day the Capitol consisted of an irregular grouping of two buildings, one medieval and the other Early Renaissance, sited at an odd angle—slightly less than a right angle—to each other. It had never had the symmetrical form that Michelangelo, brilliantly taking advantage of the odd angle of the two buildings, planned for it. By adding a third building, adapting the original two, and closing the fourth side in a balustrade with statues, he formed a piazza of greater depth than width, with matching facades to the left and right. An oval pavement with an interlacing, starlike design completes the composition. In the center stands the ancient gilded bronze statue of the Emperor Marcus Aurelius on horseback. This statue had been preserved during the Middle Ages because it was then thought, mistakenly, to represent Constantine, the first Christian emperor. If it had been known that it actually represented the pagan philosopher-emperor Marcus Aurelius, it would almost certainly have been destroyed, as were so many others, in an unfortunate excess of Christian zeal.

The piazza is reached from the lower level of the city at the foot of the hill by a wide ramplike stair on an axis with the monumental entrance designed by the artist for the Palace of the Senators at the far end of the piazza. As one walks up the easy slope of the long stair from the cramped, narrow streets of the city below, the symmetry and truly Roman scale and grandeur of the composition make it seem as if one were entering another, timeless world. The golden statue of the ancient emperor links the splendor of Imperial Rome with that of the Renaissance popes, confirming the old idea of the city, whether pagan or Christian, as eternal and universal.

The same three-dimensional imagination that gives Michelangelo's paintings their sculptural quality, and that enabled him to envision a figure within a block of marble, gave him the power to become one of the world's greatest architects. Like his painting and sculpture, his architecture is organic and dynamic. He believed that "the members of an architectural structure follow the laws exemplified in the human body." His architectural designs have the left-and-right symmetry of the human figure, with its matching pairs of eyes, ears, arms, and legs. His buildings were conceived in space and composed in the round. He used the familiar architectural elements—the columns, capitals, cornices, arches, moldings, and so on—not geometrically, by measure, as was usual, but freely, like a sculptor modeling a figure to be seen from all sides. His test as to whether or not a design was satisfactory was always a visual test: did it or did it not suit his critical eye. In this way he created new and dramatic effects of light and shade. He did this not just for surface interest, but to mold the form of his buildings as if they had evolved naturally, like crystals or seashells, by the forces of nature herself.

CHAPTER VIII

The Wonder of the World

In 1545 Michelangelo turned seventy, but he was to work steadily on St. Peter's for almost twenty more years. Every day he rode on horseback to the Vatican through the narrow medieval streets of Rome. The length of the working day depended on the number of daylight hours, so it varied with the season. But he was always there, checking with the stonecutters and carvers, the carpenters who constructed and moved the scaffoldings, the engineers who raised the blocks of shaped stone to put them in place, and the masons who secured them. He knew and oversaw each process. He often discussed practical details with the skilled craftsmen, many of whom he had personally selected. As the work progressed, he ordered full-sized wooden mock-ups of such architectural details as cornices, moldings, window frames, and columns. In this way he could be sure that the results he envisioned would be achieved. Unlike most architects, he did not trust measurement and geometrical proportion alone, but used his eye to judge the visual effect to be realized in stone. "It is necessary," he said, "to keep one's compass in one's eyes, . . . not in the hand, for the hands execute, but the eye judges."

Michelangelo spent as little time as possible with the many visitors to the vast, incomplete building, though people of position and importance, filled with curiosity and wonder, streamed through. He much preferred spending his time with the workmen, sometimes taking his meals with them. He knew that he carried in his head the only complete designs there were for the immense structure, and he was determined to see it through to completion.

Although most of his friends and relatives in Florence had died by this time, Michelangelo would doubtless have liked to return there in his old age; he was always, despite his distinguished Roman career, a loyal

Florentine. Furthermore, Cosimo de' Medici, the grand duke, offered him every inducement and paid him every honor. "But," as the artist wrote his friend Vasari, "to leave Rome now would rejoice many a scoundrel," and "ruin the whole work, a great shame to me and for my soul a great sin." He felt that to leave Rome with St. Peter's incomplete would amount to the betrayal of a sacred trust. He drove himself tirelessly.

The incomparable dome of St. Peter's crowns the composition. Seen from the air on the previous page the curving colonnaded entrance court beyond is by Bernini and was constructed in the seventeenth century.

Michelangelo's tastes were simple. He did not wish for luxury. He had a comfortable house near the Forum of Trajan in an ancient part of Rome. He had wealth enough, people to take care of him, and good friends. Whatever the weather, he took daily walks for his health's sake and to study yet again the many ruins of imperial Rome. In them he found inspiration for his own work; their grandeur of concept matched his own. He also frequently went riding in the countryside. He dressed soberly, often wearing a quilted black damask jacket. He wore soft leather boots made to his own design and a broad-brimmed felt hat. When the weather turned bad, he put on a long woolen cloak that protected him from rain and cold. He ate sparingly, enjoying pasta, fish, green salads, cheese, and good country bread, washing it down with Trebbiano, a soft Tuscan wine that friends sent him from Florence. He needed little sleep, and he often spent long evenings sitting by the fire, talking with friends, writing letters and poems, or sketching ideas for artistic or architectural projects. Among those he exchanged letters with were the king and queen of France, the grand duke of Tuscany, Cardinal Ippolito de' Medici and other Medici family members, the duke of Ferrara, popes and other churchmen, fellow artists like Vasari, and many more.

Since the accession of Pope Julius II in 1503, Rome had become recognized as the intellectual and artistic center of Europe, and since the completion of the Sistine Ceiling in 1512, Michelangelo had been established as unquestionably the leading artist in Rome. In 1547, at seventy-two, he became officially the "Supreme Architect, Sculptor, and Painter of the Apostolic Palace," the "High Commissioner and Architect of St. Peter's," and an honored "Citizen of Rome." He was the last of the three greatest figures of the High Renaissance, giants who changed the course of the arts of the Western world, and he had outlived the other two, Leonardo da Vinci and Raphael, by more than a generation. Nearly thirty years before, in 1519, Leonardo had died in France, a legendary figure full of honors, the favorite companion of King Francis I. A year later Raphael had died in Rome at the tragically young age of thirty-seven. From then on Michelangelo stood alone.

Michelangelo's redesign of the ancient Capitol (1538–64) on the Capitoline Hill in Rome created one of the world's most distinguished urban compositions, centered around the antique equestrian statue of the philosopher-emperor Marcus Aurelius.

He was surrounded by many gifted artists, but no such geniuses as these. The power of his achievement during the more than forty years that followed profoundly influenced European art for generations.

Michelangelo's last twenty years were in many ways the most richly productive and satisfactory of his long life. Many of the old self-doubts remained, but we know from his poetry that he had acquired increased confidence, hope, and faith, much of it gained through the influence of his friend Vittoria Colonna. He enjoyed a unique reputation and was admired and respected. Everyone knew him and saluted him as he rode through the streets of Rome. He was the dining companion of popes and cardinals. His advice was sought by kings and princes. He allowed none of this, however, to interfere with his work on St. Peter's, which, he believed, he was foreordained to carry out.

Inspired by Brunelleschi's much admired dome of the cathedral of Florence, Michelangelo planned "its sister" for St. Peter's, "bigger, yes, but not more beautiful," and he had a model made to illustrate his design. From his own time to ours, however, the world has considered the dome of St. Peter's the most splendid dome ever built. Though significant changes were made by other architects before the great church was finally finished, it still embodies so much of the spirit and grandeur of Michelangelo's ideas that it is truly a monument to him and to his extraordinary vision. St. Peter's is

Rondanini Pietà.

1555–64. Michelangelo never finished this work, which is named for the family that once owned it. When he had almost completed it, he suddenly, at what he called "the twenty-fourth hour of my life," radically changed the composition to unite the figures of the Virgin and her Son into a spiritual whole. The base on which the sculpture is shown is not by Michelangelo.

86

the artist's greatest architectural work and the supreme expression of the High Renaissance.

From about 1555, Michelangelo had worked on a new *Pietà*. When he couldn't sleep, Vasari tells us, he would often go into the workshop and carve the marble by the light of a lamp, and with a candle fastened to his hat. Even in his old age, he was lean and sinewy, with broad shoulders and the muscular structure of an athlete, a physique developed by the constant exercise of walking, horseback riding, and especially from wielding a sculptor's hammer. The *Pietà* was not a commission. Michelangelo was doing it entirely for himself, as an expression of the mystic faith that had grown through his relationship with Vittoria and the circle of thoughtful friends they shared. As with all his projects, the idea of the sculpture changed and evolved as the work went on.

By 1563, eight years later, the *Pietà* was nearly finished. He worked on it almost daily, and began to change the composition. As he labored through the wet and cold fall and winter, he chipped away much that he had virtually completed, including even parts that he had already polished. In spite of the weather, he went often to the Vatican to oversee the work there, yet he continued to work on the *Pietà*. At the end of January, 1564, it was still unfinished. Michelangelo spent all of February 12, Vasari recalls, chiseling away on it. By this time the figures of Christ and His mother had been transformed from solid three-dimensionality to become spirit forms. Slender and almost flame-like, they are fused together in an expression of divine love.

Two days later, though it continued to be wet and cold in Rome, Michelangelo went riding in the countryside outside the city, where he loved looking at the ruins of ancient monuments and the endless arches of the aqueducts marching across the empty landscape. The next day, in spite of a fever, he insisted, against the advice of his doctors and friends, on riding again. After that he weakened steadily. On February 18, seated in his favorite chair by the fireside, with friends around him, he dictated his will. As Vasari remembers, he was "still in perfect self-possession. . . . He left his soul to God, his body to the earth, and his goods to his nearest relatives." He died shortly before five o'clock on that rainy winter afternoon, a few weeks before his ninetieth birthday.

The next day Michelangelo's body lay in state in the church of the Holy Apostles not far from his house. For hours throngs of Romans filed past his coffin to pay their respects. As he had wished, his body was then taken to Florence by his nephew, Lionardo Buonarroti. It had to be done secretly, however, because the city of Rome wanted to keep the mortal remains of the artist who had brought it such fame and provided it with so many masterpieces.

A few days later when the coffin arrived in Florence in the evening, all the architects, artists, and craftsmen of the city escorted it by the light of torches to the artist's burial place in the church of Santa Croce, his family's parish church. Men fought for the honor of carrying his coffin. "All desired the glory," as Vasari remembered, "of having borne to earth the remains of the greatest man ever known to the arts." A state funeral attended by hundreds was conducted in the Medici church of San Lorenzo. Fittingly, this was the burial place of Michelangelo's devoted friend Lorenzo the Magnificent, whose understanding patronage had, so many years before, launched him on his career.

With Michelangelo's death an era ended. In his art he not only summed up the High Renaissance but anticipated the two styles that followed: Mannerism and the Baroque. Mannerism, which prevailed until about 1600, derives its name from the fact that during this period artists were profoundly influenced by the style or manner of the three giants of the High Renaissance: Leonardo da Vinci, Raphael, and especially Michelangelo. Michelangelo's use of light, bright colors, as in the Sistine Ceiling, and of ambiguous and crowded space and contorted figures, as in the *Last Judgment,* virtually established the Mannerist style. Mannerism didn't last long, but soon led into the prevailing style of the seventeenth century, the Baroque, a style full of animation and movement, of violent emotion and of ecstasy. In his sculpture and architecture, Michelangelo anticipated the Baroque. The style is also foreshadowed in the movement and tense drama of the *Last Judgment,* with its sense of doom. It appears in the intense awareness and feeling of taut expectancy expressed by his *David,* and in the inner turmoil and conflict of passions of his colossal *Moses* for the Julius tomb. It can be felt in the tragic expression of his first and last *Pietàs,* in the restless individualism of his design for the Laurentian Library stair, with the curiously shaped steps "flowing like lava," as one thoughtful critic observed. It appears in the soaring buoyancy of the design of St. Peter's tremendous dome.

The very size and scale of Michelangelo's ideas go far beyond the neat, finite measures of Renaissance theory and practice. In such immense compositions as St. Peter's and the Capitol he both looked forward to and provided models for the achievements of the Baroque century to come. Gianlorenzo Bernini, the most brilliant architect and sculptor of that century, summed it up when he wrote that "Michelangelo was the greatest as a sculptor and a painter, but as an architect he was truly divine."

Stone, especially the marble found in the Tuscan mountains near Florence, was Michelangelo's natural medium. He respected and was stimulated by its bulk and hardness, which reflected his own stubborn determination. When he drew, it was as a sculptor. When he painted—and he was trained first as a painter— he did it sculpturally, as may be seen in the figures on the newly cleaned ceiling of the Sistine Chapel in the Vatican in Rome. His architectural designs have a sculptural quality about them, expressed in a freely original but always monumental style that was completely his own. His poetry, and he was perhaps the leading Italian poet of his time, has the same craggy individuality. Everything he created has a heroic and larger-than-life quality that reflects the grandeur of the vision that he sought to realize. But even his almost superhuman powers could rarely express to his own complete satisfaction the magnitude of his ideas, so demanding was his drive toward perfection. As he once wrote to a friend, "God is perfection, and whoever strives toward perfection is striving for something divine." Michelangelo spent his long and wonderfully rich life in pursuit of that ideal.

Daniele da Volterra.
Michelangelo.
1565. This bronze portrait bust was sculptured by a devoted friend and loyal follower of Michelangelo.

List of Illustrations

PAGE 43: *David* (detail of face).
Photo: Alinari

PAGE 44: Raphael. *Pope Julius II* (detail of *Mass at Bolsena*). 1512. Fresco. The Vatican, Rome.
Photo: Canali

PAGE 47: *Ceiling of the Sistine Chapel.* 1508–12. Fresco, 130'6" x 43'5" (entire ceiling). The Vatican, Rome.
Photo: Nippon Television Corporation, Tokyo

PAGE 48: *Studies for the Libyan Sibyl.* 1511. Red chalk on paper, $11^3/_8$ x $8^3/_8$". The Metropolitan Museum of Art, New York, Purchase, 1924, Joseph Pulitzer Bequest

PAGE 49: *Head Study for Leda.* 1529–30. Red chalk, 14 x $10^5/_8$". Casa Buonarroti, Florence

PAGES 51–52: *Adam and Eve in the Garden of Eden* (detail of ceiling of the Sistine Chapel).
Photo: Nippon Television Corporation, Tokyo

PAGES 53–56: *Ceiling of the Sistine Chapel* (half cleaned, half uncleaned).
Photo: Nippon Television Corporation, Tokyo

PAGES 57–58: *The Creation of Man* (detail of ceiling of the Sistine Chapel).
Photo: Nippon Television Corporation, Tokyo

PAGE 60: *Tomb of Pope Julius II.* Completed in 1545. Church of San Pietro in Vincoli, Rome.
Photo: Alinari

PAGE 63: *Moses* (detail of head). c. 1513–16. Marble, height: $92^1/_2$". Church of San Pietro in Vincoli, Rome. Photo: Anderson/Alinari

PAGE 64: View of Medici Chapel with Tomb of Lorenzo and Madonna. 1519–34. The Medici Chapel, Florence. Photo: Brogi/Alinari

PAGE 65: *Madonna and Child.* The Medici Chapel, Florence. Marble, height: $7'5^3/_8$".
Photo: Brogi/Alinari

PAGE 66: *Night* (detail of Tomb of Giuliano de Medici). Marble, height: $6'4^3/_4$".
Photo: Gabinetto Fotografico della Sopraintendenza alle Gallerie, Uffizi

PAGE 67: Tomb of Giuliano de Medici. 1519–34. Marble. The Medici Chapel, San Lorenzo, Florence. Photo: Anderson/Alinari

PAGE 69: *The Last Judgment.* 1536–41. Fresco, 48 x 44' (approx.). The Sistine Chapel, The Vatican, Rome. Photo: Canali

PAGE 70: *Brutus.* c. 1540. Marble, height: $29^1/_2$". Museo Nazionale, Florence. Photo: Alinari

PAGES 72–73: Staircase of Laurentian Library. Begun in 1524, completed in 1559. San Lorenzo, Florence. Photo: Alinari

PAGE 74: *Conversion of St. Paul* (detail).
Photo: Vatican Archives

PAGE 75: *Conversion of St. Paul.* 1542–45. Fresco, 20'4" x 22'. Pauline Chapel, The Vatican, Rome.
Photo: Alinari

PAGES 76–77: *Martyrdom of St. Peter.* 1545–50. Fresco, 20'4" x 22'. Pauline Chapel, The Vatican, Rome. Photo: Alinari

PAGE 78: *Deposition* (detail of *Self-Portrait as Joseph of Arimathea*).
Photo: Gabinetto Fotografico della Sopraintendenza alle Gallerie, Uffizi

PAGE 79: *Deposition.* c. 1550–55. Marble, height: 7'8". Duomo Cathedral, Florence.
Photo: Alinari

PAGE 80: Project and Plan for St. Peter's. 1546–54. The Vatican, Rome

PAGES 82–83: St. Peter's (view from air).
Photo: Alinari

PAGE 84: St. Peter's (west view).
Photo: Canali

PAGE 85: The Capitol, Rome. 1538–64.
Photo: Alinari

PAGE 86: *Rondanini Pietà.* 1555–64. Marble, height: $63^3/_8$". Castello Sforzesco, Milan.
Photo: Eugenio Cassin Editore, Florence

PAGE 89: Daniele da Volterra. *Bust of Michelangelo.* 1565. Bronze. Museo Nazionale, Florence.
Photo: Alinari

ENDSHEETS: Florentine School. *Bird's-eye view of Renaissance Florence.* c. 1450. Woodcut. The Metropolitan Museum of Art, New York. The Elisha Whittelsey Fund, The Elisha Whittelsey Collection, 1959. 59.508.1

Index